EVERY MOMENT BECOMES A MEMORY.

I0432544

EVERY MOMENT BECOMES A MEMORY.

NEVER STOP BEING AMAZED.
THERE IS ALWAYS SOMETHING NEW TO DISCOVER.

PROGRESSION AND ACCEPTANCE

RELAX. MEDITATE. ONENESS. FOCUS.

RELAX. MEDITATE. ONENESS. FOCUS.

BE EASY ON YOURSELF.

A MOVEMENT IS BUILT IN MORE THAN ONE DAY.

A MOVEMENT IS BUILT IN MORE THAN ONE DAY.

GO SLOW. BE CAREFUL.

PRECISION. DEDICATION. EXCELLENCE.

DON'T CALL THE POLICE, CALL UPON PEACE.

EVOKE MOMENTS OF AWE.

HUMANS HAVE HIGHER THINKING FOR A MULTITUDE OF REASONS,
WHAT IS YOUR REASON TO UTILIZE YOUR BRAIN?

LIVING HAS TRANSFORMED ITSELF INTO AN ART.

LEVELS OF DEDICATION:
INDIFFERENT, CURIOUS, INTRIGUED, INTERESTED, ENGAGED,
INVESTED, INTENSITY, OBSESSION, DEVOTION

LOGIC. ORDER. REASON.

LOGIC. ORDER. REASON.

FILL THESE PAGES WITH DREAMS AND PASSIONS,
THEN DO THEM.

DON'T CRATE, CREATE.

BEING HUMAN ISN'T COMFORTABLE.

BEING HUMAN ISN'T COMFORTABLE.

ACTIVELY LISTEN TO OTHERS.
THINK & DECIDE FOR YOURSELF.

BE AN ADVENTURE.

EXPERIENCE. REMEMBER. RECORD.

BE A SKEPTIC & STILL BELIEVE IN MAGIC.

STAY OPTIMISTIC.

BE POSITIVE.

KEEP SMILING.

ACT ETHICALLY ALWAYS.

LOOK WHERE YOU ARE GOING
SEE WHERE YOU HAVE BEEN

FIND THE BALANCE BETWEEN:
INTELLECT & ACADEMIA
PLANNING & PROCEEDING
STABILITY & SPONTANEITY

DO NOT ERASE MEMORIES, EMBRACE THEM.

UNIVERSAL TRUTH & BEAUTY

BE THE PERSON YOU'VE DREAMED OF BEING.

ALWAYS ASK: WHY?

KNOW WHY OR WHY NOT.

FIND THE BALANCE BETWEEN THINKING ABOUT DOING AND JUST DOING.

INCREASE BRAIN CAPACITY

NEVER STOP LEARNING.

NEVER BE BORED.

EVERYTHING IS INTERESTING.
LOOK CLOSER.

COMPILE. ORGANIZE. ARTICULATE.

ENERGIZED. INVIGORATED.

DILIGENCE. DETERMINATION. RESOURCEFULNESS.

MAKE & CHASE OPPORTUNITIES.

STRIVE. PURSUE. ACHIEVE. THRIVE.

ENJOY NOW.

MAKE AND SHARE.
SOMEONE IS WAITING TO FIND THE WORDS
TO DESCRIBE WHAT THEY ARE GOING THROUGH,
THIS IS THROUGH YOUR SHARED EXPERIENCES.

YOU CAN DO ANYTHING.
MOST PEOPLE ARE WILLING TO HELP.

DO NOT WASTE TIME OR BRAIN SPACE.

DEVOTE YOURSELF TO MEANINGFUL & PRODUCTIVE ACTIVITIES.

APPROACH PROJECTS WITH DEDICATION & CONVICTION.

IF YOU COULD HAVE WHATEVER YOU WANT...
...WHAT WOULD BE WHATEVER YOU WANT BE?

EVERYDAY THERE IS A DIFFERENT ANSWER TO LIFE.

DON'T LIVE OTHER PEOPLE'S DREAMS,
FIND YOUR OWN.

DEVELOP LIFE-LONG ACTIVATES NOW
GIVE YOURSELF SOMETHING TO FEEL NOSTALGIC ABOUT.

THE SECRET TO MAKING ART IS TO NOT THINK
ABOUT WHY YOU ARE MAKING, WHERE IT WILL GO, OR IF IT IS GOOD ENOUGH.
JUST MAKE, KNOWING THAT YOUR WHOLE LIFE HAS PREPARED YOU FOR THIS MOMENT.
AND IN THIS MOMENT, YOU DO NOT NEED TO THINK.
YOU DO NOT NEED PERMISSION.
SIMPLY ACT.
CREATE.
DO.
GO.
BE.
MAKE.

www.ingramcontent.com/pod-product-compliance
Lightning Source LLC
Chambersburg PA
CBHW082344220526
45470CB00008B/2631